I0017311

Revealing the **secrets** of

Cybersecurity:

Protecting Your Digital World

Professor Rodríguez

Title: Revealing the Secrets of Cybersecurity: Protecting Your Digital World

Collection: From zero to ninety

© Luis Rodríguez Domenech, 2024

All rights reserved.

The content of this book is protected by intellectual property rights. Except as provided by law, reproduction, distribution, public communication, or transformation without the authorization of the rights holder is a violation punishable by law.

To my mother, for her infinite love and dedication.

Índice

Preface

The digital era has brought countless benefits and technological advancements that have improved our lives in ways we couldn't even imagine a few years ago. However, it has also led to an increasing number of threats and vulnerabilities in cybersecurity.

In our current world, where information is just a click away, it is vital to protect our privacy and ensure that our personal and professional data is safe from *cybercriminals*. The simple act of using the internet and electronic devices exposes us to risks that can jeopardize not only our information but also our identity and finances.

That is why I decided to write this book: "***Revealing the Secrets of Cybersecurity: Protecting Your Digital World***" Our goal is to provide you, as the reader, with the knowledge and tools necessary to protect your information and stay safe in the digital world.

We hope you enjoy reading and that this book provides you with the necessary tools to protect your digital world. Together, we can face the challenges of *cybersecurity* and stay one step ahead of cybercriminals.

This book is the first in the "***From zero to ninety***" collection. A collection that aims to instruct our readers on various computer topics in an easy and quick way, using simple language and summarizing the extensive content that exists on these subjects as much as possible.

Why *From zero to ninety*? Because our goal is to provide you with the maximum amount of information possible in the shortest amount of time for each topic our books cover. We want to take you from zero to ninety percent of the knowledge on a subject, and you, dear reader, contribute the remaining ten percent with your interest in learning in this passionate and exciting world of computer science.

Welcome to *Revealing the Secrets of Cybersecurity: Protecting Your Digital World*!

Introduction

In the current digital era, it is more important than ever to protect your identity and data online. With the rise of cybercrime, it is crucial that we take steps to safeguard our personal and professional information. Whether you are a business owner or an individual, it is important to understand the basics of cybersecurity. In this book, we will reveal the secrets of cybersecurity, explore the major online threats and techniques used by cybercriminals to access people's systems and data, and provide practical tips on how to protect your digital world. We will explore different types of cyber threats, discuss the importance of password management, highlight the benefits of using a _VPN_, and offer guidance on how to detect _phishing_ scams. We will examine the topic of online privacy and the implications of sharing personal information on social networks and other websites. We will teach you how to navigate the internet safely and protect your electronic devices from _malicious attacks_. By the end of this book, you will have the knowledge and tools necessary to protect your online presence from potential threats.

It is important to note that cybersecurity is not solely the responsibility of technology experts. We all need to be aware of the risks and take measures to avoid becoming victims of cybercriminals. We firmly believe that everyone can learn to protect their digital world, and for that reason, this book has been written with all types of readers in mind, from beginners to advanced users.

There is no reason to panic or fear the existing online threats. Instead, we invite our readers to take control and become experts in cybersecurity. Through the basic concepts and strategies presented in this book, you will be able to make more informed decisions and establish secure practices to protect your information and privacy.

1 The importance of cybersecurity in the digital era

In the current world of technology, _cybersecurity_ has become more important than ever. As technology continues to advance at an unprecedented pace, so do the _threats_ and _risks_ that come with it. From _hackers_ and **cybercriminals** to _data leaks_ and _identity theft_, the digital world is a minefield of potential dangers.

Cybersecurity refers to the measures and practices implemented to protect sensitive information and ensure the _integrity, confidentiality, and availability_ of data. It encompasses a wide range of areas, including **network security**, **data protection**, _encryption_, _access control_, and incident response.

The importance of cybersecurity cannot be underestimated. A single security breach can result in significant **financial losses**, **damage to reputation**, and **legal consequences**. With the growing dependence on digital platforms for communication, transactions, and the storage of personal and business data, what's at stake is greater than ever.

Protecting your digital world begins with understanding the risks and taking proactive measures to mitigate them. This includes implementing strong passwords, regularly updating software and systems, using robust _antivirus_ and _firewall_ protection, and educating yourself and your team on safe online practices. It also entails staying informed about the latest security threats and adopting a proactive approach to addressing them.

Investing in cybersecurity measures is not only a wise decision, but also necessary in today's interconnected world. By prioritizing the protection of your _digital assets_, you can safeguard your personal information, business data, and the trust of your clients. Remember, **the cost of preventing a security breach is much lower than the cost of addressing its consequences.**

2 Understanding the Threats to Your Digital World

In today's interconnected world, understanding the threats to your digital world is vital. As technology advances, so do the tactics used by cybercriminals. It is essential to stay informed and take preventive actions to protect your valuable digital assets.

One of the most common threats is _malware_, malicious software designed to infiltrate and damage your computer systems. This can take various forms, including _viruses_, _worms_, _ransomware_, and _spyware_. Malware can spread through infected email attachments, malicious websites, or even unsuspecting downloads. It can wreak havoc on your data, compromise your privacy, and disrupt your operations.

Another significant threat is _phishing_, where cybercriminals attempt to deceive people into providing confidential information such as passwords or credit card data. They often impersonate trusted entities and use convincing emails, websites, or phone calls to deceive unsuspecting victims. Falling for a phishing scam can result in **identity theft**, **financial losses**, or **unauthorized access** to your accounts.

Hackers are also a persistent threat. These skilled individuals exploit vulnerabilities in your network or systems to gain unauthorized access. They can take advantage of **weak passwords**, **outdated software**, or unpatched _security vulnerabilities_ to breach your defenses. Once inside, hackers can **steal confidential information**, **disrupt services**, or even **take control of your systems**.

Social engineering is another tactic used by cybercriminals to manipulate people into revealing confidential information. This can involve tricking someone into disclosing passwords, granting access to secure areas, or unknowingly downloading malware. Social engineering attacks often rely on psychological manipulation, exploiting human tendencies such as trust or curiosity.

Understanding these threats is the first step in protecting your digital world. By knowing the tactics used by cybercriminals, you can take **preventive measures** to safeguard your data and systems. Implementing strong security measures such as **firewalls, antivirus software**, and **encryption** can help fortify your defenses. Regularly updating your software, using strong and *unique passwords*, and educating yourself and your employees on **cybersecurity best practices** are crucial to mitigating these risks.

Remember, the digital landscape is constantly evolving, and **new threats periodically emerge**. Stay informed, stay vigilant, and invest in the appropriate security measures to safeguard your digital world. By doing so, you can minimize the risk of falling victim to cyber threats and protect your valuable assets.

3 Common Vulnerabilities in Online Environments

At the current moment of the digital revolution, where information and data are constantly shared and stored online, it is crucial to be aware of common vulnerabilities that exist in online environments. By understanding these vulnerabilities, you can take proactive measures to protect your digital world.

One of the most common vulnerabilities is **weak passwords**. Many people tend to use simple and easy-to-guess passwords, such as birth dates, pet names, or even "123456". Hackers can easily crack these passwords, leaving your accounts and confidential information exposed. It is important to create strong and unique passwords that include a combination of uppercase and lowercase letters, numbers, and symbols.

Another common vulnerability is outdated software. Software developers regularly release *updates and patches* to fix bugs and security vulnerabilities. Not updating your software leaves your devices and systems susceptible to attacks. Always make sure to install the latest updates for your operating system, web browsers, and any other software or applications you use.

Phishing attacks are also a frequent vulnerability in online environments. These attacks involve cybercriminals attempting to deceive people into revealing their personal information, such as passwords or credit card details, by pretending to be trusted entities through fake emails, messages, or websites. It is essential to be cautious and skeptical of any unsolicited email or message that requests personal information. Double-check the sender's email address and verify the legitimacy of any website before entering confidential data.

Furthermore, insecure Wi-Fi networks pose a significant vulnerability. When connecting to public Wi-Fi networks, such as those in cafes or airports, hackers can intercept your data. Avoid accessing sensitive information or conducting financial transactions while connected to a public Wi-Fi network. Instead, use a virtual private network (VPN) to encrypt your internet connection and ensure your data remains secure.

Lastly, ***improper data backup practices*** can leave you vulnerable to data loss and ransomware attacks. Making ***regular*** *backups* of your important files and data on an ***external hard drive***, ***cloud storage***, or other secure locations can prevent the devastating consequences of data loss.

By being aware of these common vulnerabilities, you can take proactive steps to protect your digital world. Implementing secure passwords, keeping your software up to date, being cautious of phishing attempts, securing your Wi-Fi connections, and making regular data backups are essential steps to safeguarding your online environments.

4 Strengthen your passwords and authentication measures

In today's world of digital communication, where our personal and sensitive information is stored and accessed online, it is absolutely crucial to strengthen our passwords and authentication measures to protect our digital world. Hackers and cybercriminals are constantly evolving and finding new ways to violate security systems and gain unauthorized access to our accounts.

One of the simplest yet most effective ways to enhance password security is to create strong and unique passwords for each of our online accounts. Gone are the days of using predictable passwords like "123456" or "password". Instead, **opt for complex combinations of uppercase and lowercase letters, numbers, and special characters**. The longer and more complex your password, the harder it will be for hackers to decipher.

Additionally, it is crucial to avoid using the same password for multiple accounts. This is because if one account is compromised, all other accounts also become vulnerable. Using a *password manager* can be incredibly helpful in generating and securely storing unique passwords for each account, eliminating the need to remember them all.

In addition to strong passwords, implementing _multifactor authentication_ (MFA) adds an extra layer of security. MFA requires users to provide two or more forms of identification to access an account, such as a password and a unique verification code sent to their smartphone. This significantly reduces the risk of unauthorized access, even if a password is compromised.

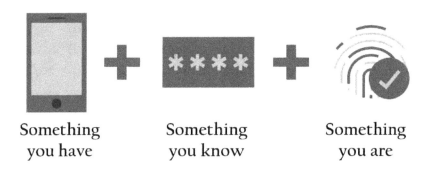

MULTI-FACTOR AUTHENTICATION

Something you have   Something you know   Something you are

Regularly updating passwords and reviewing authentication measures is equally important. Set reminders to change passwords periodically, especially for critical accounts like email and banking. **Stay informed** about the latest security practices and technologies, as cyber threats constantly evolve.

By strengthening your passwords and authentication measures, you reinforce the walls that protect your digital world. Remember, taking some extra steps to improve security today can save you from potential cyber disasters in the future.

5 The Role of Encryption in Protecting Your Data

In today's interconnected world, where digital data is constantly transmitted and stored, the importance of encryption in protecting your data cannot be overstated. **Encryption** acts as a safeguard by transforming your data into an unreadable format that can only be deciphered with the correct encryption key.

One of the main benefits of encryption is its ability to ensure confidentiality. By encrypting your sensitive information, such as personal data, financial transactions, or intellectual property, you can prevent unauthorized individuals from accessing and understanding the data. Even if a malicious party manages to intercept the encrypted data, without the encryption key, it would be virtually impossible for them to make sense of it.

Furthermore, encryption plays a crucial role in maintaining data integrity. With encryption in place, any alteration or manipulation of the data during transmission or storage will render it useless, as the *encryption algorithms* will detect the changes and the decryption process will fail. This provides an additional layer of protection against unauthorized modifications or unauthorized access to your data.

Moreover, **encryption is essential for ensuring data authenticity**. By using digital signatures, encryption allows for verification of the origin and integrity of the data. *Digital signatures* use cryptographic algorithms to create a unique identifier for the data, which can be verified with the corresponding *digital certificate*. This ensures that the data has not been tampered with and originates from a trusted source.

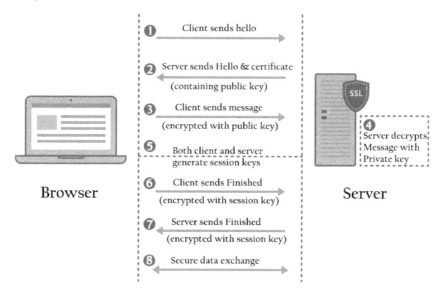

The implementation of encryption technologies, such as *Secure Socket Layer* (SSL) or *Transport Layer Security* (TLS), is essential for protecting confidential data during transmission over networks, such as the internet. These protocols encrypt the data and establish encrypted connections between the client and server, preventing unauthorized access and eavesdropping.

In conclusion, **encryption is a vital component of computer security**, acting as a strong barrier against unauthorized access, ensuring data integrity, and verifying data authenticity. By implementing encryption measures, individuals and organizations can protect their digital world and safeguard their confidential information from potential threats and cyber attacks.

6 Best practices for secure online navigation and communication

In the current stage of digital transformation, where almost every aspect of our lives is intertwined with the Internet, it is more crucial than ever to prioritize the security of our online activities. Whether you are browsing the web or communicating with others, following best practices for secure online navigation and communication can help protect your digital world.

First and foremost, it is essential to keep software and devices updated with the latest security patches. Software developers frequently release updates to address vulnerabilities and enhance overall security. By periodically updating your operating system, web browsers, and applications, you ensure that you have the strongest protection against potential threats.

When browsing the internet, exercise caution with the websites you visit. Stick to trustworthy and reputable sites, especially when sharing sensitive information or conducting online transactions. Look for the padlock symbol in the URL bar, indicating that the website has a *valid SSL certificate*, encrypting your data and protecting it from interception.

Another important practice is to be mindful of the links you click on. Phishing attacks remain a common threat, where cybercriminals disguise *malicious links* as legitimate ones to deceive unsuspecting users. Always hover your cursor over a link before clicking on it to verify its destination, and be wary of unsolicited emails or messages requesting personal information.

Using strong and unique passwords for all your online accounts is a fundamental aspect of secure online navigation. Avoid using easily guessable passwords and consider using a password manager to generate and store complex passwords for you. Additionally, enabling two-factor authentication whenever possible adds an extra layer of security by requiring a verification code in addition to your password.

When it comes to online communication, encrypted messaging apps provide an additional level of privacy and security. Apps like **Signal** and **WhatsApp** utilize *end-to-end encryption*, ensuring that only the intended recipient can access your messages.

Lastly, it is crucial to stay informed about the latest cybersecurity threats and keep up-to-date on evolving security practices. Stay primarily updated on topics such as phishing scams, malware attacks, and social engineering techniques. By staying informed, you will be better able to protect yourself and your digital world from potential security breaches.

By following these best practices for secure online navigation and communication, you can strengthen your defenses against cyber threats and enjoy a safer and protected digital experience. Remember, safeguarding your digital world is an ongoing effort that requires diligence and awareness, but the peace of mind it brings is undoubtedly worth it.

7 Protecting your devices and networks

Protecting your devices and networks is essential in today's digital world. With the increasing cyber threats, it is crucial to take anticipated actions to protect your confidential information and personal data.

Firstly, make sure that all your devices, including smartphones, tablets, laptops, and desktop computers, are equipped with up-to-date antivirus software. This software acts as a shield against malicious software such as viruses, malware, and spyware that can compromise your devices and steal your data.

Additionally, regularly update your operating system and applications. Software updates often include security patches that address vulnerabilities discovered by developers. By keeping your devices up to date, you minimize the risk of falling victim to cyber attacks.

Protecting your home or office network is equally important. Change the default passwords of your routers and Wi-Fi networks to secure and unique passwords that are hard to guess. Enable encryption on your Wi-Fi network to ensure that data transmitted between devices and the network is encrypted, making it difficult for hackers to intercept and decipher.

Consider implementing a firewall to monitor and control incoming and outgoing network traffic, providing an additional layer of protection. Firewalls help detect and block unauthorized access attempts, preventing potential attacks.

Another crucial step is **to regularly backup your data**. Whether through cloud storage or external hard drives, creating backups of your important files ensures that even if your devices are compromised, you can restore your data and minimize the impact of a possible cyber attack.

It is also essential to educate yourself about common cyber threats such as phishing scams and social engineering. Be cautious when clicking on links or downloading attachments from unknown sources, and be wary of unsolicited emails or messages requesting personal information.

Remember, protecting your devices and networks is an ongoing process. Stay vigilant, keep your software updated, and follow best practices to safeguard your digital world from potential threats.

8 The importance of software updates and patches

In today's digital world where cyber threats constantly evolve and become more sophisticated, the importance of software ***updates and patches*** cannot be emphasized enough. These updates and patches play a crucial role in protecting your digital world from various vulnerabilities and security breaches.

Software developers work continuously to identify and fix any flaws or weaknesses in their software. Hackers can exploit these vulnerabilities to gain unauthorized access to your devices or confidential data. By regularly installing software updates and patches, you ensure that you have the latest security enhancements and bug fixes, effectively closing any possible loopholes in your system.

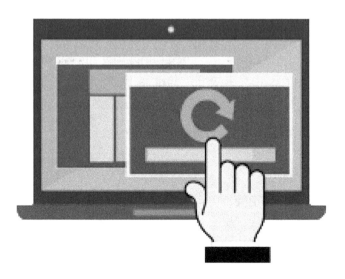

One of the main reasons why software updates are so important is because they often address known security vulnerabilities. As new threats arise, developers release updates to fix these vulnerabilities and protect your devices and data. Without these updates, you are essentially leaving your digital world exposed to potential attacks.

Furthermore, software updates not only enhance security but also improve overall performance and functionality of your software. They can introduce new features, fix bugs, and optimize software performance, providing you with a smoother and more efficient user experience.

It is worth noting that software updates are not limited to *operating systems* only; they also apply to applications and other software installed on your devices. Failing to update these applications can leave them vulnerable to attacks, as hackers often target known vulnerabilities in popular software.

In conclusion, regularly updating your software and applying patches is a vital part of maintaining a solid and secure digital environment. By staying up-to-date with the latest updates and patches, you ensure that your devices, data, and digital world remain protected against emerging threats, giving you peace of mind in an increasingly interconnected world.

9 Educate yourself and your loved ones about online safety

In this hyperconnected world we live in, it is crucial to prioritize online safety for yourself and your loved ones. As cyber threats become increasingly sophisticated, educating yourself about online safety is key to safeguarding your digital world.

Start by staying informed about the latest trends and techniques used by hackers. Follow reputable sources and security blogs that provide information about emerging threats and best practices for protection. By understanding the tactics employed by cybercriminals, you will be better able to anticipate and prevent potential attacks.

Additionally, educate your loved ones, including family members, friends, and colleagues, about the importance of online safety. Raise awareness about common cyber risks such as phishing scams, identity theft, and malware. Encourage them to practice safe browsing habits, such as *avoiding suspicious websites* and *not clicking on unknown links or downloading files from untrusted sources*.

Teach them the importance of strong and unique passwords, emphasizing the use of a combination of uppercase and lowercase letters, numbers, and special characters. Stress the importance of regularly updating their software and operating systems to ensure they have the latest security patches.

It is also essential to instill a habit of skepticism when interacting with online content. Remind your loved ones to think twice before sharing personal information or conducting online transactions. Encourage them to verify the authenticity of websites and the credibility of sources they come across online.

By educating yourself and your loved ones about online safety, you will create a strong defense against potential cyber threats. Together, we can create a safer digital world and protect our valuable information from falling into the wrong hands.

10 Create a strong backup and recovery strategy

Creating a solid *backup* and recovery strategy is crucial to protect your digital world. In today's fast-paced, technology-driven society, we heavily rely on information and digital data. From important documents and financial records to precious memories captured in photographs, the loss of such data can be devastating.

To ensure the protection of your valuable information, it is essential to have a comprehensive backup and recovery plan. This involves creating redundant copies of your data and storing them in *secure locations separate from your main system*. By doing so, you mitigate the risk of permanent data loss in the event of hardware failure, cyber attacks, or natural disasters.

There are several backup solutions available, ranging from external hard drives and _network-attached storage (NAS)_ devices to cloud-based services. Each option has its own advantages and considerations, so it is important to choose the one that best suits your needs and budget.

When designing your backup strategy, it is crucial **to establish a regular schedule** for data backups. Depending on the frequency of data changes and the importance of the information, you can opt for daily, weekly, or even real-time backups. Additionally, it is recommended to perform **periodic test restores** to ensure the integrity and accessibility of your backups.

Equally important is the recovery aspect of your strategy. In the unfortunate event of data loss or system failure, a well-defined recovery plan will allow you to quickly restore your information and resume your operations. This includes **documenting the necessary steps** and procedures to recover from different scenarios, as well as identifying the necessary resources and the personnel responsible for the recovery process.

Remember, a strong backup and recovery strategy is not a one-time task, but an **ongoing commitment to the security** and continuity of your digital world. By taking proactive measures to protect your data, you can safeguard your valuable information and minimize the potential impact of unforeseen events.

11 The future of cybersecurity and emerging threats

As our world becomes increasingly digital, the future of cybersecurity poses exciting possibilities and immense challenges. With each technological advancement, new threats emerge that test the limits of our defenses and push us to adapt and innovate.

One of the most concerning trends in the future of cybersecurity is the rise of _cyber warfare_. As nations become more dependent on _digital infrastructure_, the possibility of cyber attacks disrupting _critical systems_ and causing widespread chaos is a pressing concern. From **ransomware attacks** targeting hospitals to state-sponsored hacking attempts on government networks, what is at stake is greater than ever.

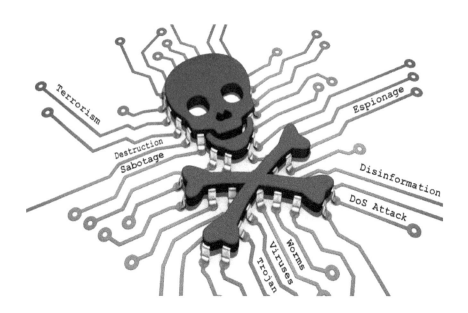

Another emerging threat is the growing sophistication of _artificial intelligence_ (AI) in cyber attacks. Hackers are leveraging **AI algorithms** to automate and enhance their attacking capabilities, making it increasingly difficult for traditional security measures to detect and respond in real-time. As AI continues to advance, we must stay one step ahead, harnessing the power of AI for defensive purposes and developing robust AI-based security systems.

The _Internet of Things_ (IoT) also presents a unique set of challenges for cybersecurity. With billions of interconnected devices, from smart appliances to industrial control systems, the attack surface for cybercriminals expands exponentially. Weaknesses in IoT devices and networks can be exploited to gain **unauthorized access** or launch large-scale _DDoS attacks_, highlighting the need for stringent security measures and industry-wide standards.

In addition to these technical threats, the human factor remains a significant vulnerability. **_Social engineering_** attacks, such as phishing and _spearphishing_, continue to deceive unsuspecting individuals, compromising their personal and professional data. Educating users about potential risks, implementing strong authentication protocols, and fostering a cybersecurity-aware culture are crucial in mitigating these threats.

Looking towards the future, it is clear that cybersecurity will be an ongoing battle. However, with preventive strategies, collaboration among industry experts, and continuous research and development, we can strive to stay ahead of emerging threats and protect our digital world. By embracing innovation, adopting robust security practices, and fostering a culture of cybersecurity awareness, we can navigate the evolving cybersecurity landscape and safeguard our digital future.

12 Taking control of your digital world: practical measures to improve security

In a world where technology has become an integral part of our daily lives, it is crucial to take control of our digital world and prioritize the security of our personal information. Protecting ourselves from online threats and maintaining a safe digital environment requires proactive measures and increased awareness of potential risks.

To improve your security and safeguard your digital assets, here are some practical steps you can follow:

1. Strengthen your passwords: create unique and complex passwords for all your online accounts. Avoid using easily guessable information and consider using a password manager to securely store your passwords.

2. Enable two-factor authentication (2FA): Two-factor authentication adds an additional layer of security by requiring an additional verification step, such as a unique code sent to your mobile device, when logging into your accounts.

3. Keep software and devices up to date: regularly update your operating system, applications, and antivirus software. These updates often include security patches that address vulnerabilities and protect against emerging threats.

4. Be cautious of phishing attempts: be wary of opening emails, clicking on links, or downloading attachments from unknown sources. Watch out for signs of phishing attempts, such as suspicious email addresses, grammatical errors, and requests for personal information.

5. Secure your home network: change the default username and password of your Wi-Fi router, enable encryption (WPA2 or WPA3), and periodically check for unauthorized devices connected to your network.

6. Backup your data: regularly backup your important files and documents to an external storage device or a cloud-based service. In the event of data loss or a security breach, having backups ensures you can recover your information.

7. Practice safe browsing habits: use secure and encrypted websites (look for "*https*" in the URL), avoid clicking on suspicious ads or pop-ups, and use a reputable antivirus or browser extension that can detect and block malicious websites.

8. Educate yourself and your family: stay informed about the latest security threats and educate yourself and your family members about best practices for online security. Teach children about the importance of protecting personal information and the potential risks of oversharing online.

By implementing these practical steps, you can take control of your digital world and significantly improve your security. Remember, digital security is an ongoing process, so stay vigilant and adapt to new threats as they arise. Protecting your digital assets and personal information is crucial in today's interconnected world.

Conclusions

Computer security is an increasingly important concern in our digital lives, and it is essential to take measures to protect our personal information and devices. Education and awareness are key to protecting oneself in the digital world. It is crucial to understand the risks and follow best security practices. This responsibility extends not only to individual users but also to companies and organizations, who should implement appropriate security measures to safeguard their customers' confidential information.

Furthermore, computer security is a constantly evolving field, with new threats and vulnerabilities emerging continuously. It is crucial to stay updated on the latest trends and technologies in computer security and continuously adapt protection measures accordingly. Ultimately, *computer security is a balance between convenience and safety*. It is important to find the right balance to protect our information without sacrificing ease of use and convenience in our digital lives.

We hope you have found our book on computer security useful and informative. In the current digital era, it is more important than ever to protect our digital world from various threats. By following the secrets revealed in this book, you will be able to take proactive steps to safeguard your personal and confidential information. Remember, the security of your digital world is in your hands, *so stay vigilant*, implement strong security practices, and stay informed about the latest security trends and technologies. Together, we can create a safer digital environment for everyone. ***Stay safe, stay protected!***

Glossary

Cybersecurity: It refers to the protection of digital information and computer systems against threats, attacks, and unauthorized access. It involves implementing measures and mechanisms to prevent, detect, and respond to security incidents that may compromise the integrity, confidentiality, and availability of an organization's data and resources. Cybersecurity encompasses various dimensions and aspects, such as designing secure networks and systems, using technical measures like firewalls, antivirus, and data encryption, implementing security policies and procedures, raising awareness and training users on good security practices, and responding to and recovering from security incidents. The main objective of cybersecurity is to ensure the trust and protection of information and computer systems, preventing theft, unauthorized manipulation, or disclosure of data, as well as damages or disruptions to an organization's services and operations.

Threats: It refer to any type of action or event that jeopardizes the security of computer systems, such as cyberattacks, intrusions, information theft, among others.

Risks: They are situations that may cause harm to cybersecurity, such as human errors, system failures, natural disasters, among others.

Integrity, confidentiality, and availability: They are the three fundamental pillars of cybersecurity. Integrity refers to the guarantee that data has not been modified in an unauthorized manner; confidentiality refers to keeping data protected and accessible only to authorized individuals; and availability refers to systems being accessible and functional when needed.

Encryption: It is a process used to convert readable data into unreadable data, with the aim of protecting confidential information during transmission or storage.

Access control: It refers to the measures implemented to limit and control who can access computer systems and resources.

Malware: It is a general term used to refer to any type of malicious software, such as viruses, worms, trojans, spyware, among others.

Viruses: They are a type of malware that spreads autonomously and can cause harm to the infected system.

Worms: They are computer programs that spread through the network, mainly by exploiting vulnerabilities in systems to infect other devices.

Ransomware: It is a type of malware that hijacks a user's files or system and demands a ransom in exchange for their release.

Phishing: It is a social engineering technique used to deceive users and obtain confidential information, such as passwords, through identity theft.

Security vulnerabilities: They are flaws or weaknesses in computer systems that attackers can exploit to compromise security.

Social engineering: It is a technique used to manipulate people and obtain confidential information or unauthorized access to systems or networks.

Firewall: It is a security barrier used to filter and control network traffic, allowing or denying access based on predefined rules.

Backup: It is a security measure that involves making copies of important data and files to be able to recover them in case of loss or damage.

Multifactor authentication: It is a security method that requires two or more forms of identity verification, such as a password and a verification code sent to a phone.

Digital signature: It is a cryptographic mechanism used to ensure the integrity and authenticity of a document or message.

Digital certificate: It is an electronic document that certifies the authenticity of a person, company, or entity's identity, used in the field of cybersecurity, especially in encryption and secure connection authentication.

Secure socket layer: SSL is a security protocol used to establish a secure connection between a client and a server over the internet.

Transport layer security: TLS is the successor to the SSL protocol and is used to ensure security in communications over the internet.

End-to-end encryption: It is an encryption technique that protects data from the point of origin to the destination point, so that only the sender and the receiver can access it.

Updates and patches: They are software updates released regularly to correct vulnerabilities and enhance the security of operating systems and programs.

Operating system: It is the main software that allows the management and control of computer resources and the execution of other programs.

Cyber warfare: It refers to the use of cyberattacks as a form of conflict between nations or groups.

Critical systems: They refer to systems that are crucial for the security and operation of an organization or country, such as energy systems, transportation, communications, among others.

Artificial intelligence: It is a field of computer science that focuses on developing systems and programs capable of performing tasks that require human intelligence, such as learning, decision-making, and pattern recognition.

Internet of Things: It refers to the connection and communication between physical objects through the internet. These objects, which can be appliances, vehicles, electronic devices, sensors, among others, are equipped with technology and the ability to collect and transmit data. The IoT allows these objects to connect and share information with each other, creating an intelligent network in which the collected data can be used to make decisions and improve the efficiency and functionality of the systems.

DDoS attacks: They are distributed denial-of-service attacks, where multiple devices are used to flood a system or network with a high volume of requests, overwhelming it and making it inaccessible to legitimate users.

Cybercriminal: It is a person who commits computer or cyber crimes using technology and resources available in the digital environment. These criminals employ their technical skills to access, manipulate, damage, or steal information in computer systems and networks, or to engage in illegal online activities such as fraud, identity theft, cyber espionage, harassment, phishing, distribution of malware, among others. Their main objective is to obtain economic benefits, acquire confidential information, or cause harm or damage to others.

VPN: (Virtual Private Network) It is a technology that allows for the creation of a secure and encrypted connection between a device and a private network over the internet. The main purpose of a VPN is to provide privacy and security to users by transferring their data through a virtual tunnel. This is achieved by encrypting the transmitted information and hiding the actual IP address of the device, replacing it with the IP address of the connected VPN server.

Spearphishing: It is a social engineering tactic used by cybercriminals to deceive specific individuals and obtain confidential information such as passwords, banking data, or other personal information. Unlike conventional phishing, spearphishing is more sophisticated and targeted, as attackers research specific targets to personalize email messages, text messages, or social media messages to make them appear legitimate and persuasive. The intention is for the target person to click on malicious links, download infected attachments, or provide their personal data, which can lead to compromised information systems or information theft.

Malicious attacks: They are actions carried out by individuals or groups with the intention of damaging or compromising a system or a computer network. These attacks can have various motivations, such as obtaining confidential information, disrupting the normal functioning of a system, or causing financial harm. Some examples of malicious attacks include phishing, malware, ransomware, hacking, spoofing, among others. These attacks can result in the loss of important data, the theft of personal or financial information, the paralysis of a system or network, or unauthorized access to protected resources.

Antivirus protection: It is a term used to describe a series of measures and tools designed to protect computers and other electronic devices from possible threats of malware and computer viruses. These measures can include antivirus programs, firewalls, antispyware software, and other security solutions that help prevent, detect, and eliminate viruses and other types of threats in real time. The main goal of antivirus protection is to maintain the integrity and security of computer systems, protecting information and avoiding any potential damage that cyber threats may cause.

Digital assets: They are virtual or digital representations of a physical or intangible asset. They are electronic files that contain information and can represent different forms of value, such as digital currency, intellectual property rights, virtual goods, or any other type of intangible asset. Digital assets can be stored, transferred, and managed on digital platforms like blockchain, which is a technology that guarantees the security, transparency, and decentralization of information.

Unique passwords: It refers to the practice of using different passwords for each account or online service that a person has. Instead of using the same password for multiple accounts, unique passwords require each account to have its own exclusive password. The objective of this practice is to minimize the risk of an attacker gaining access to multiple accounts if one password is compromised. By using unique passwords, the scope of a possible attack is limited, as even if one account is breached, the others will remain secure because they use different passwords. It is an important measure to protect the security of accounts and personal data.

Password Manager: It allows users to generate secure and unique passwords for each account, store them in an encrypted database protected by a master password, and auto-fill login credentials on different websites and applications.

Encryption algorithms: They are mathematical or logical procedures used to transform data or information into an unintelligible format, called encrypted text, in order to protect its confidentiality and prevent unauthorized access. These algorithms apply a series of specific steps or rules, using keys or passwords, to transform the original plain text into encrypted text, which can only be reversed to its original form through a decryption process with the appropriate key. Encryption algorithms have wide uses in information security, such as password encryption, secure communication online, secure access to sensitive data, and protection of confidential files. Their objective is to maintain privacy and confidentiality of protected information.

Malicious links: They are URL links that point to harmful content or represent a threat to computer security. These links are often used by cybercriminals to deceive users and lead them to fraudulent websites, where they can become victims of scams, phishing attacks, malware downloads, or other illicit activities. Malicious links are often distributed through phishing emails, text messages, social networks, contaminated advertisements, or messages in forums and blogs. They often present themselves as legitimate and trustworthy links, but their real purpose is to harm users who access them.

Hackers: They are individuals or groups of people who use advanced technical skills to gain unauthorized access to computer systems and networks, with the aim of stealing, modifying, or destroying confidential information, as well as disrupting or damaging the normal operation of such systems and networks. Often, hackers seek to obtain economic benefits, such as stealing financial information or blackmailing organizations or individuals, but they can also act for political, ideological, or simply entertainment purposes. The act of hacking is illegal and can have serious legal consequences for the perpetrators.

Data leaks: They refer to the unauthorized or accidental disclosure of confidential or sensitive information to unauthorized individuals or entities. This can occur due to security breaches, failures in computer systems, human errors, or malicious actions. These leaks can involve the exposure of personal or financial data, trade secrets, confidential information of companies or governments, passwords, or any other type of sensitive information. The unauthorized disclosure of this data can have serious consequences, such as identity theft, financial fraud, damage to a company's reputation, or even threats to national security.

Identity theft: It is a crime in which a person uses someone else's personal information, without their consent, in order to commit fraudulent or illegal activities. This involves unauthorized access to someone's personal information, such as their name, social security number, credit card number, address, among others, to obtain economic benefits or commit fraud in their name. Identity theft can manifest itself in different ways, such as fraudulent use of credit cards, opening fake bank accounts, filing false tax returns, applying for loans or lines of credit in the victim's name, among other forms of fraud. In addition to causing significant financial damage, it can have an emotional and psychological impact on the victim, affecting their reputation and even making it difficult to obtain employment or financial services in the future.

Spyware: It is a type of malicious computer program designed to infiltrate a device without the knowledge or consent of the user, for the purpose of collecting personal or confidential information. Spyware can gain access to a wide range of data, such as passwords, browsing history, emails, instant messages, call logs, saved files, and can even activate the camera/webcam and microphone of the device to record activities without consent. This type of program is often used illegally or unethically for information theft, espionage, fraud, or surveillance without consent.

Network-Attached Storage (NAS): It is a storage solution that consists of an independent device connected to a local area network (LAN) that allows users to access and share files centrally through the network. A NAS is equipped with one or multiple hard drives and uses its own network interface to connect and communicate with other devices on the network, such as computers, printers, security cameras, among others. The main advantage of a NAS is its ability to provide centralized and shared storage, allowing multiple users to access the same files and data from different devices and locations. This is especially useful for collaborative work environments and homes with multiple devices.

Digital infrastructure: It refers to the set of systems, networks, and technologies that enable the communication, processing, and storage of digital information. It consists of hardware, software, communication networks, and related services used to facilitate data transfer and access to information. Digital infrastructure includes elements such as servers, networking equipment, cabling, network management software, storage systems, and data centers, among others. These components are essential for the operation of information and communication technologies (ICT), as they enable fast and reliable data transmission, as well as efficient processing and storage of information. Additionally, digital infrastructure also encompasses the services and applications developed on this technological foundation, such as websites, e-commerce platforms, cloud services, mobile applications, among others. These applications and services rely on digital infrastructure for their operation and access.

About the author

The author is a professional in the field of IT and communications with over 25 years of experience. He has worked as a telecommunications technician, hardware technician, system administrator, and cybersecurity specialist. He has been involved with companies in various sectors such as tourism, software programming, cybersecurity, maritime transport, and public health. He has also taught courses and workshops on various topics, including network administration and web application security. He promotes the use of open-source software in both applications and operating systems. He has experience managing heterogeneous network environments with interoperability between Windows, Linux, Unix, and other operating systems. With over 10 years of experience in cybersecurity and ethical hacking, he has provided network security and web application consulting to companies of all sizes, from local small businesses to large corporate groups.

He now offers his knowledge and experience gained through research, teaching, and years of professional career, with the desire to provide useful knowledge and help professionals improve or simply provide readers with a general understanding of some of the most current topics in the IT world.

📣 Feedback

Dear reader, we hope that this book has been useful and has allowed you to gain clarity and knowledge on this interesting and exciting topic of **Cyberecurity**. Our intention is for this book to be in constant evolution and also to create others that are more specific on many of the topics we have covered here, that is what the "_From zero to ninety_" collection is all about. Your suggestions on topics of your interest or any other concerns you would like to raise will be very useful to us. To do so, you can contact us through the following channels:

 _easycomputing4everyone@gmail.com_

 _easycomputing4everyone_

www.ingramcontent.com/pod-product-compliance
Lightning Source LLC
LaVergne TN
LVHW051622050326
832903LV00033B/4623